Biblical Church Discipline

Daniel E. Wray

Pastor of
Limington Congregational Church
Limington, Maine

THE BANNER OF TRUTH TRUST

The Banner of Truth Trust
The Grey House, 3 Murrayfield Road, Edinburgh EH12 6EL
P.O. Box 621, Carlisle, Pennsylvania 17013, U.S.A.

*

First Published 1978
Reprinted 1981

ISBN 0 85151 269 0

Introduction

It is necessary in our hardened and apostate age for the church to be called back to the New Testament doctrine of church discipline. In our day, the church has become tolerant of sin even when it is found in her own people. This warrants the wrath of God upon the church's indifference to his holiness. The modern church seems more willing to ignore sin than to denounce it, and more ready to compromise God's law than to proclaim it. It is a mournful fact that many churches refuse to take sin seriously. We have no right to dialogue about sin. That was Eve's mistake. The tempter's suggestions should have been promptly rebuked; but instead, they were discussed [*Gen* 3:1–5]. That discussion was compromise and sin. The church cannot stand before her enemies while ignoring sin in her own ranks [cf. *Joshua* 7: 1–26].

Today, the church faces a moral crisis within her own ranks. Her failure to take a strong stand against evil (even in her own midst), and her tendency to be more concerned about what is expedient than what is right, has robbed the church of biblical integrity and power. It is true that, historically, the church has sometimes erred in this matter of discipline, but today the problem is one of outright neglect. It would be difficult to show another area of Christian life which is more commonly ignored by the modern evangelical church than church discipline.

It is ironic that this rejection is often justified in the name of love. When the apostle John wrote that we should 'love one another', he also wrote: 'And this is love, that we walk after his commandments.' [2 *John* 5, 6]. As we shall see, the exercise of church discipline is a command from the Lord of the church. When it is properly carried out, it is a profound display of Christian love. To put it another way, true Christian love dare not ignore the use of the various forms of discipline wherever they are applicable. Love necessarily challenges sin in ourselves and in our brethren. It is no more love for a Christian to watch a brother in Christ pursue a course of sin unchallenged than it is love for a parent to watch his child walk unhindered into disaster. If we look for God's blessing in our churches, it is essential that we conduct ourselves according to God's Word. He tells us how to conduct ourselves in 'the house of God' [1 Tim 3:15]. We must not look to the world for such guidance. If we are to practise Christian love, we must practise church discipline. On the other hand, it will do the church no good if we practise the proper forms of discipline without the spirit of love and humility which characterizes disciples of the Lord Jesus Christ. We do not intend to suggest that church discipline is a cure-all for the ills of the contemporary church; nor that discipline is the only or the chief way in which we ought to display our love for one another. Rather we advocate that this is part of the reform necessary in the church today. The way to reform in the church always lies along the road of biblical revelation. The purpose of this booklet, therefore, is simply to point the way back to the biblical practice of church discipline.

The following outline will make our approach plain: (1) The *necessity and purpose* of church discipline; this will answer the question. 'Why practise it?'. (2) The *modes* of church discipline; this will answer the question, 'How do we discipline?'. (3) The *proper recipients* of church discipline; this will answer the question, 'Who should be disciplined?'. (4) Anticipated *objections* to church discipline and our answers to them.

1. Necessity and Purpose

Just as the church applies biblical principles in admitting persons to membership, so too must she apply biblical principles in the governing of the membership and, if necessary, in removal from membership. Jesus prescribed principles to follow which make all Christians to some extent responsible for each other's behaviour, and he included disciplinary procedures [Matt 18:15–17].

2

It is in this context that he gave the church the responsibility to pronounce his forgiveness and his judgments. 'Verily I say unto you, Whatsoever ye shall bind on earth shall be bound in heaven: and whatsoever ye shall loose on earth shall be loosed in heaven.' [*Matt* 18:18]. Of course, the ratification in heaven of what the church does on earth is contingent upon the church acting in obedience to Christ and his principles without hypocrisy or favouritism. As Matthew Poole puts it, this text is 'to assure stubborn and impenitent sinners that he would ratify what his church did, according to the rule he had given them to act by. It is therefore a terrible text to those who are justly and duly cut off from the communion of the church . . .' Poole wisely adds: 'The church is not by this text made infallible, nor is the holy God by it engaged to defend their errors.' The only fact to be established at this point, however, is simply that the Lord Jesus Christ *does* indeed intend his church to govern its members even to the extent of disciplinary measures when these become necessary. Let us not think that this is simply an optional power to act, for all of the Lord's instructions are given in the imperative. The church does not have the right to ignore persistent sinful behaviour among its members. Our Lord has not left that option open to us.

The necessity and purpose of church discipline can be readily exhibited in six particulars:

1. To glorify God by obedience to his instructions for the maintenance of proper church government. God's Word makes it plain that he intends discipline of various types to be a part of church life [*Matt* 18:15–19; *Rom* 16:17; 1 *Cor* 5; 1 *Thess* 5:14; 2 *Thess* 3: 6–15; 1 *Tim* 5:20, 6:3; *Tit* 1:13, 2:15, 3:10; *Rev* 2:2, 14, 15, 20]. It is always glorifying to God when we obey his Word rather than cater for our own ease and expediency. Let us not be as those in Jeremiah's day, of whom it is written: 'The word of the Lord is unto them a reproach; they have no delight in it' [*Jer* 6:10].

2. To reclaim offenders. The goal in every type of discipline,

whether it be gentle correction, admonition, rebuke, or excommunication, is always the restoration of the offender. [*Matt* 18: 15; 1 *Cor* 5:5; *Gal* 6:1] None of the biblical instructions in this matter *promise* that restoration will result. Nevertheless, God's wise directions as to how a sinner is to be brought to repentance are to be respected and obeyed. Thus, while we might be inclined simply to pray about the matter, God commands action to accompany our prayers. The apostle's instructions concerning an offender, 'count him not as an enemy, but admonish him as a brother', [2 *Thess* 3:15] set the tone for this grievous work. As Calvin observes: 'Although excommunication also punishes the man, it does so in such a way that, by forewarning him of his future condemnation, it may call him back to salvation.' (*Institutes*, Bk. IV, Ch. 12, Sec. 10).

3. To maintain the purity of the church and her worship [1 *Cor* 5:6–8], and to avoid profaning the sacrament of the Lord's Supper [1 *Cor* 11:27]. We shall never be able to keep the visible church in perfect purity since we are but fallible men. Our inability to achieve perfection in this matter, however, is no excuse for giving up the attempt. We must maintain the purity of Christ's visible church to the full extent of our knowledge and power. This is all the more evident once we recognize that false doctrine and bad conduct are infectious. If these are tolerated in the church all members will receive hurt.

4. To vindicate the integrity and honour of Christ and his religion by exhibiting fidelity to his principles [2 *Cor* 2:9, 17]. The church which refuses to exercise discipline can neither command the world's respect nor the confidence of its own members.

5. To deter others from sin [cf. 1 *Tim* 5:20]. By the faithful practice of discipline, 'vice is repressed and virtue nourished' (*The Scots Confession* (1560) Ch. XVIII).

6. To prevent giving cause for God to set himself against a local church (see *Rev* 2:14–25).

Since the church is bound to give full allegiance to the Lord Jesus Christ and this means to love him and keep his commandments [*John* 14:15, 23, 24; 15:10, 14], it is evident that the church's honesty of heart is tested when confronted with the choice between obedience and disobedience in this matter of the discipline of its members. It is just as necessary for the church to exercise proper discipline as it is to preach the Word and properly administer the sacraments. This is why the *Belgic Confession* (1561), which grew out of Reformation soil, says: 'The marks by which the true Church is known, are these: if the pure doctrine of the gospel is preached therein; If she maintains the pure administration of the sacraments as instituted by Christ; if church discipline is exercised in punishing of sin; in short, if all things are managed according to the pure Word of God, all things contrary thereto rejected, and Jesus Christ acknowledged as the only Head of the Church.' (From Chapter XXIX. A similar statement can be found in Chapter XVIII of *The Scots Confession*: (1560).

2. Modes

The modes or types of church discipline vary from the mild to the severe. The following are biblical:

1. Admonition – either private or public [*Rom* 15:14; *Col* 3:16; 1 *Thess* 5:14; 2 *Thess* 3:14, 15; *Tit* 3:10, 11]. The *Oxford English Dictionary* defines 'admonish' as 'to put (one) in mind *to do* a duty; to charge authoritatively, to exhort, to urge (always with a tacit reference to the danger or penalty of failure).' The Scripture itself is a form of admonition [1 *Cor* 10:11]. Christians ought to admonish and encourage one another, for example, to do good works and to attend the meetings of the church [*Heb* 10:24, 25].

2. Reprove, rebuke, convince, convict [*Matt* 18:15; *Eph* 5:11; 1 *Tim* 5:20; 2 *Tim* 4:2; *Tit* 1:9, 13, 2:15] The Greek word (elenchō), which is used in the passages just cited, is a rich word which means '. . . to rebuke another with such effectual wielding of the victorious arms of the truth, as to bring him, if not always

5

to a confession, yet at least to a conviction, of his sin . . .' (R. C. Trench, *Synonyms of the New Testament*, p. 12). This word is also used of the Holy Spirit's work in *John* 16:8, and is found on the lips of the enthroned Christ in *Revelation* 3:19, where he says: 'As many as I love, I rebuke and chasten: be zealous therefore, and repent'. Thus, proper rebuke is an act of love. The proper guide in such matters is the Word of God which we are told is 'profitable . . . for reproof' [2 *Tim* 3:16].

It is important that all Christians practise loving admonition and rebuke in their relationships one with another. Many a Christian has been prevented from more serious misbehaviour or error by the gentle rebuke of a brother in Christ. If Christians would conscientiously apply admonition and rebuke, there would be less need for excommunication. Knowing this, the faithful Christian is eager to help turn sinners to repentance before excommunication becomes necessary. Furthermore, Christians will help one another 'grow up into him in all things' if they will obey the apostle's admonition to be 'speaking the truth in love' [*Eph* 4:15].

As each Christian gives thought to his responsibility here, let it always be remembered that the only proper source of admonitions and rebukes is the Word of God. This does not mean that we must always quote Scripture to one another, but it certainly does mean that the substance of all admonitions and rebukes must be soundly and clearly scriptural. We are not to offer one another human ideas; but rather, are to speak with the authority of 'Thus saith the Lord'. This should be done in humility, remembering that we ourselves are nothing but sinners saved by grace. Furthermore, repentance and faith constitute the way of salvation for all Christians; thus we attempt to lead the sinner on the same path which we ourselves must tread. We do not stand over them as superiors, but beside them as brothers [*Gal* 6:1–3; 2 *Thess* 3:15].

3. Excommunication. The descriptions given by our Lord Jesus Christ and the apostle Paul define this final form of discipline: '. . . if he neglect to hear the church, let him be unto thee

as an heathen man and a publican' [*Matt* 18:17]; 'But now I have written unto you not to keep company, if any man that is called a brother be a fornicator, or covetous, or an idolater, or a railer, or a drunkard, or an extortioner; with such an one no not to eat . . . Therefore put away from among yourselves that wicked person' 1 *Cor* 5:11, 13]. Thus this most severe of the forms of discipline excludes the offender from the church and from all the privileges of membership. However, while the person must certainly be excluded from the Lord's Supper, he is not excluded from attendance upon the ministry of the Word preached and taught, for even non-believers are welcome to the public assemblies [1 *Cor* 14:23–25]. That this form of discipline is unpleasant and a cause for mourning [1 *Cor* 5:2] none would doubt. Nevertheless, this practice has associated with it in the New Testament Christ's own direct sanction [*Matt* 18:18, 19]. Paul claims this sanction when he writes concerning the Corinthian situation that the man is to be delivered to Satan (i.e. put back into the world which is Satan's domain), 'in the name of our Lord Jesus Christ' and 'with the power of our Lord Jesus Christ' [1 *Cor* 5:4]. He could hardly state more clearly and decisively that our Lord Jesus himself is the authority behind true excommunication.

It is not to be thought that excommunication is irreversible, for the person who repents of his sin and seeks God's cleansing and pardon is to be welcomed back into the fellowship of the church [2 *Cor* 2:6–8]. Indeed, it is the responsibility of God's people to continue to pray for any persons thus removed from fellowship that God will bring them to repentance. On the other hand, so long as they remain unrepentant they remain excommunicated. We recognize, of course, that in this day and age the offender will often seek out another church to attend in order to avoid repenting and submitting to the church which loved him enough to discipline him. In such cases, the offender and the other church must answer to God. The disciplining church, if it has done its duty well, will be vindicated by the Lord in his own time. (Cf. Objection 8, page 14.)

In view then of the severity of a sentence of excommunication, it must be asked what offences would warrant the use of this extreme censure.

3 Proper Recipients

The church has both the responsibility and the authority to be involved with the doctrine and the conduct of its members. To belong to the church requires adherence to the doctrines and standards of conduct required in the Scriptures. True disciples of Christ are always under his discipline which he administers in many ways, chiefly through the church and its duly appointed officers. The very Scriptures themselves are to be an instrument of discipline [2 *Tim* 3:16], and should be taught 'with all authority' [*Titus* 2:15].

All breaches of the biblical standards of doctrine and behaviour require some form of discipline. Thus, every believer needs to be disciplined, and 'whom the Lord loves, he disciplines' [*Heb* 12:6]. This does not mean, however, that Christians may leave all disciplining to the Lord, thus forsaking their own responsibilities to one another. We do not have the right to overlook clear violations of Christian love, unity, law, and truth. Therefore, church discipline is necessary when:

1. Christian love is violated by serious private offences. Jesus prescribes the method of discipline in such cases in Matthew 18:15–18. Though such offences may begin in secret, they must ultimately result in public censure if the offender stubbornly refuses to repent. Such refusal to repent and be reconciled is a severe aggravation of the sin involved and a continual breach of Christian love.

2. Christian unity is violated by those who form divisive factions which destroy the peace of the church. Such persons must be watched, rebuked, and, if necessary, removed [*Romans* 16:17, 18; *Titus* 3:10].

3. Christian law is violated by those living scandalous lives.

8

Such are those who 'profess that they know God; but in works they deny him' [*Titus* 1:16]. Biblical Christianity undeniably teaches a high standard of conduct and morality. The New Testament's ethical instructions are many – *Matt* 15:19, 20; *Rom* 13: 8–14; *Eph* 4:25–6:8; *Col* 3:5–4:6; 1 *Thess* 4:1–10; 2 *Tim* 3:22–4:5; *Tit* 2:1–3:3 – to mention only a few. Those who live in habitual violation of biblical morality, and refuse to repent when admonished and rebuked, must be removed from church membership [1 *Cor* 5].

4. Christian truth is violated by those who reject essential doctrines of the faith [1 *Tim* 1:19, 20, 6:3–5; 2 *John* 7–11]. This does not mean that Christians should be censured for failing to understand and receive every doctrine revealed in the Bible, for all Christians are learning and growing. Rather, this refers to those who knowingly reject any of those doctrines which the church considers essential and fundamental. In the case of the pastors and elders of the church, the standard is more rigid, since they are especially responsible to teach and defend 'all the counsel of God' [*Acts* 20:27]. Thus they are responsible to maintain all the doctrines of the Scripture (especially as embodied in their church's creed), and are liable to discipline if they fail to do so [1 *Tim* 3:2, 9; *Titus* 1:9; *James* 3:1].

In each case, the cause of further discipline is impenitence. The person who will not repent of his sin is not living like a Christian. Only the repentant sinner can be counted as holy in Christ, and only the holy in Christ have a place in the fellowship of the saints (i.e. holy ones), as members of Christ's church. Therefore, regardless of what the offender's sin(s) might be, it is ultimately his impenitence that must exclude him from the church. *Repentant* sinners, who 'bring forth fruit in keeping with repentance' [*Matt* 3:8], are what the church is made of. This is why Martin Luther wrote in the first of his Ninety-Five Theses (1517); 'Our Lord and Master Jesus Christ, in saying "Repent ye, etc.," meant the whole life of the faithful to be an act of repentance.' There is no place for the impenitent, who are treasuring up 'wrath against the day of wrath' [*Rom* 2:5]. Even the religious activities of the unrepentant are worthless and abominable to God [*Prov* 15:8; 28:9, *Amos* 5:21–27; *Malachi* 2:11–14].

4. Objections and Questions

Whenever the Church attempts to be faithful to the biblical directions concerning discipline, a multitude of objections is sure to arise. John Calvin was well aware of this when he wrote in the sixteenth century:

'But because some persons, in their hatred of discipline, recoil from its very name, let them understand this: if no society, indeed, no house which has even a small family, can be kept in proper condition without discipline, it is much more necessary in the church, whose condition should be as ordered as possible ... Therefore, all who desire to remove discipline or to hinder its restoration, whether they do this deliberately or out of ignorance, are surely contributing to the ultimate dissolution of the church. For what will happen if each is allowed to do what he pleases? Yet that would happen, if to the preaching of doctrine there were not added private admonitions, corrections, and other aids of the sort that sustain doctrine and do not let it remain idle.' (*Institutes*, Bk. IV, Ch. XII, Sec. 1).

Many people mistakenly think that once a biblical teaching is established, they need only raise a few objections against it to overthrow it. This is not the case. The only objections which can overthrow a doctrine are those which overthrow the facts on which it is based. None of the following objections can do that. Nevertheless, many Christians encounter genuine problems in the realm of church discipline. Therefore, as a help to the sincere questioner, we offer the following answers to some common objections and questions:

1. *Objection:* 'The practice of discipline could cause divisions'.

Answer: Yes it could; but so could preaching the Bible consistently (cf. Luke 12:51–53)! The fact is that obedience to Christ and his Word is more important than an artificial 'unity' built on disobedience and compromise. If discipline is carried on decently and in order, with the church acting through its duly appointed officers, divisions should be kept to a minimum.

2. *Objection:* 'To discipline someone would be "judging" them'.

Answer: If guilt is clearly established (as is essential), then the person has judged himself. As long as he refuses to repent he continues to pronounce himself guilty. In discipline the church does not determine a judgment, but only pronounces the judgment of Christ upon the person who insists on bearing his own guilt. Paul rebukes the Corinthians for failing to do this [1 *Cor* 5:1, 2] and the Lord Jesus similarly rebukes the church in Thyatira [*Rev* 2:20]. There is a great difference between the right act of judging of 1 Corinthians 5:3, 4 and the wrong act of judging of Matthew 7:1-5.

3. *Objection:* 'We are all sinners ourselves, so how can we condemn another?'

Answer: This objection is similar to the previous one. Yes, we are all sinners ourselves, sinning every day in thought, word and deed. If we were persisting in open sin without repentance, remorse, or desire to change, we would be subjects for discipline also. Again, the point is that we ourselves condemn nobody. We only pronounce Christ's judgment upon those who bring this censure upon themselves by persisting in sin without repenting. Such impenitence is inconsistent with a Christian profession of faith (see again the final paragraph of Section 3).

4. *Objection:* 'If our Christian leaders and friends intend to practise discipline, we will find ourselves unable to trust them in confidence with any sin-problems we might have'.

Answer: Hopefully we can always trust our Christian leaders, brothers, and sisters to be faithful to Christ. If they are faithful to Christ they will certainly be faithful to the best interests of his people. If you go to a Christian friend to ask his help to conquer a sin into which you have fallen you obviously expect that he will not betray your trust. On the other hand, if you display persistent sinful behaviour, and have neither intention nor desire to be delivered from the sin, then certainly discipline is required despite pleas of violated confidentiality and trust. In the latter case the purity of God's church is being violated and his name profaned, and the individual's very soul destroyed because no one will confront him with his sin, and call him back to repentance. Is confidentiality or even friendship more important than those reasons named in Section I for the necessity of discipline? By no means!

5. *Objection:* 'Church discipline (especially excommunication) seems unloving. Would it not be more loving to work patiently with the offender and try to lead him gradually out of his sin without resort to discipline?'

Answer: Certainly if progress is visible, as a person is confronted and biblically counselled about his sin, then that procedure should be continued. If there is no visible progress in the form of repentance, or at least a professed desire to overcome the sin, then the church has no authority to continue hoping for deliverance without discipline. Compromise or toleration of overt and continual sin is not an option for God's people. To continue a process of *talk* with a person who has made his intention to continue in sin clear, is a failure to *act* biblically. It betrays the extent to which humanistic psychological theory has become authorative in our churches. As G. I. Williamson so aptly put it: 'Lack of church discipline is to be seen for what it really is – not a loving concern as is hypocritically claimed, but an indifference to the honour of Christ and the welfare of the flock' (*The Westminster Confession of Faith for Study Classes, p.* 237).

6. *Objection:* 'Does not the phrase "against you" [*Matt* 18:15] *limit* disciplinary procedures to be followed to the one who is inned against?'

Answer: By no means, because:

a. Every sin, if persisted in without repentance, is a sin first of all against Christ and then against his church, as well as against any specific individuals involved. Therefore, more is at stake than the feelings of the one currently sinned against (cf. Ps. 51:4).

b. To limit Christ's message in the way suggested would be to turn his teachings here into an absurdity. For if *only* the one sinned against is entitled to pursue discipline, then if persons outside the church are sinned against there is no recourse, because a non-believer would not be allowed to pursue a disciplinary process within God's church. Thus, whenever a brother sinned against his non-Christian neighbour, the church could do nothing about it, since no one within the church was sinned 'against'. What a dishonour that would be to the church's Lord!

c. If pastors and elders are to 'rule' God's church [1 *Tim* 3:5, 5:12; *Heb* 13:7, 17, 24], they must be entrusted with certain disciplinary powers. Ought a pastor to serve communion to a person who is known to be living in sin? Certainly not! But if the pastor has no right to proceed with discipline simply because he personally was not sinned against, then his hands are tied in such a way as to render him unable to fulfil his God-appointed responsibility to govern the church and guard the flock of God. In the Old Testament, priests had power to exclude the unclean [*Lev* 13:5; *Num* 9:7; 2 *Chron* 23:19] and were held responsible when they failed to do so. If the angels of the seven churches in *Rev* 2 and 3 are pastors, as many think, then they are especially rebuked for failing to lead in the exercise of discipline.

d. The power of binding and loosing is given to the church [*Matt* 18:18], not to the individuals sinned against. The church must pronounce God's judgment faithfully even though it hurts the feelings of the offender. The integrity and purity of God's church demand it.

e. Comparing Matthew 18:15 with other scriptures we find that in no other text is the right to exercise discipline limited to offended persons. Is the offended one mentioned in *Rom* 16:17; or 1 *Cor* 5, or 2 *Thess* 3:14?

f. Persons sinned against may or may not be mature Christians, and may or may not be leaders in the church. If they are not mature in Christ, or adequately instructed in the Scriptures, they may (in keeping with the spirit of the age) fail to see the necessity of discipline. The integrity of the church in its obedience to

Christ must, in such cases, be maintained by those appointed to rule who ought to know the Scriptures and thus the value and necessity of discipline.

g. If we were to conclude that the one sinned against is the only one who can pursue the disciplinary process, then we would also have to conclude that this person would be under divine mandate to follow-through with discipline, since the instructions in Matthew 18:15–17 are in the form of command and not of option.

7. *Objection:* 'Who is to decide how much time is to be allowed between each of the steps prescribed in Matthew 18: 15–17?'

Answer: The obvious fact is that somebody *must* decide. Jesus gives no prescription as to how much time is to be allowed between each step; hence we must assume that those closely involved in the disciplinary process must trust the Spirit of Christ to lead them. However, to prevent extreme subjectivety, their chief criterion must be the presence or absence of *visible* progress, or *visible* responsiveness to admonition and rebuke. In other words, they must ask what visible effect the Word of God is having on the offender. Does he show signs of hardening or softening as God's Word is applied to him? Church officers cannot make critical decisions on the basis of what is not visible, therefore they must proceed beyond admonition and rebuke when these produce no visible results.

8. *Objection:* 'Why proceed with public censures if the offending member decides to pull out of the church in order to avoid them?'

Answer: a. A man should not be allowed to lessen the judgment against himself for his course of sin by committing another sin (i.e. leaving the church without proper cause and becoming a schismatic) to minimize the force of such a judgment.

b. The integrity of Christ's church must be maintained both against *internal* and *external* criticisms for winking at sin. To allow a quiet withdrawal can only be construed as 'sweeping sin under the carpet'.

c. Discipline, according to biblical revelation (as we saw in Section I), is necessary for the benefit of the offender because being followed by the loving admonitions and prayers of the whole congregation, it may lead him to repentance. Christ and the apostles clearly attribute an efficacy or power to the church acts of discipline [*Matt* 18:18; 1 *Cor* 5:4, 5]. The failure to administer discipline is equivalent to a tacit admission that there is no spiritual power or authority in the act, but simply a breaking of outward ties.

d. Excommunication forewarns of the future and final judgment of God upon the unrepentant person, a judgment which none can escape by quiet withdrawal. (This further serves to deter others from sin.)

e. To allow a quiet withdrawal would be to seek peace through compromise rather than obedience. This is a worthless type of peace.

f. A church has a duty to other Christian churches not to allow a person to leave its membership in apparently good standing when it is known that that person is living in sin. This might not have been a problem in first-century Corinth, but it is a very real one today. No Christian church has the right to forsake its responsibilities to other Christian churches. If another church, knowing that a certain person is under discipline, proceeds to receive that person into fellowship, their sin will be upon their own heads. On the other hand, if one church allows an unrepentant sinner to withdraw quietly, and then that person joins another church, the first church (which failed to discipline) is responsible for allowing the corruption of another church, when it might have been prevented by the proper action of the first church.

9. *Objection:* 'I just cannot agree with casting people out of church for every little sin. Won't this turn us all into policemen?'

Answer: People are not cast out for 'little' sins but, for hardened impenitence in their sin. Nor are we to be looking for sins in other people's lives. Such a mentality is distorted and unloving. If this subject is treated with the biblical faithfulness which we have tried to display here, there should be no such abuses as this objection suggests.

10. *Objection:* 'We believe that no true Christian can lose his salvation. Does not excommunication imply a loss of salvation?'

Answer: Not necessarily. In excommunicating a person, the church is not passing judgment on the offender's ultimate salvation. As we observed before (see pp. 3-4), the long-range goal of discipline is the offender's salvation. It is true, as *The Westminster Confession* states, that Christians 'may, through the temptations of Satan and of the world, the prevalency of corruption remaining in them, and the neglect of the means of their preservation, fall into grievous sins; and for a time continue therein: whereby they incur God's displeasure, and grieve His Holy Spirit; come to be deprived of some measure of their graces and comforts, have their hearts hardened, and their consciences wounded; hurt and scandalize others, and bring temporal judgments upon themselves' (Chap XVII, Sec. 3). However, if such an offender is a true Christian to start with, he will be finally brought to repentance and be saved. On the other hand, the offender's profession of faith may not have been real to start with [*Matt* 7:21-23; 13: 1-30; 2 *Cor* 13:5; 1 *Jn* 2:19; 2 *Pet* 1:10]. In cases such as this, the church, in excommunication, has only finally exposed the hypocrisy or self-deception of the offender. Either way, it is *not* the church's prerogative to judge the category into which a particular offender fits. The example of David stands to remind us how badly a true man of God can fall (2 *Sam* 11, cf. his prayer of repentance, *Ps.* 51), while the life of Judas reminds us how close a man may seem to be to Christ and yet perish.

There is no doubt that the human mind is capable of contriving scores of objections against God's Word. We believe, however, that the chief ones have been here anticipated and answered fairly.

11. *Question:* 'How and when are offenders to be restored to the fellowship of the church?'

Answer: It has already been stated that restoration is the most desirable result of discipline [*Matt* 18:15; *Gal* 6:1]. Anyone who goes about to practise any of the modes of discipline without earnestly desiring the true repentance and forgiveness of the offender, is attempting to serve God with a false heart. Love delights in seeing sinners restored.

As the final occasion for discipline is lack of repentance, so the occasion of restoration is the presence of repentance. Such repentance may reveal itself at any stage in the disciplinary process. How happy is the Christian who finds, after a private confrontation and rebuke, that the offender has taken the faithful words of the admonitor to heart and has truly turned from his sin. In such a case he has won the brother [*Matt* 18:15]. God may be pleased to 'grant repentance' [2 *Tim* 2:25] at any of the stages referred to in section two above. When such repentance is evident on the part of the offender, there must be a corresponding visible evidence of forgiveness and full restoration on the part of those Christians (whether one or many) who have participated in the disciplinary action. This cannot be over emphasized. Failure here is critical in that it is a tacit denial of the love of the brethren, and of the free justification which we all share in the Gospel. 'And be kind one to another, tenderhearted, forgiving one another, even as God for Christ's sake hath forgiven you' [*Eph* 4:32]. On this matter see especially 2 Corinthians 2:5–11.

12. *Question*: 'What should be done if there is doubt about the genuineness of the offender's repentance?'

Answer: We should not easily allow ourselves to doubt another's repentance unless we have compelling reasons for such doubt. We are not to be judges of hearts, but only of behaviour. On the other hand we are not obliged to accept every claim of repentance without questions. When a disciplinary situation has gone beyond private admonition and has come to involve the church officers or even the whole assembly, a certain degree of caution should be exercised before total restoration. The repentant offender may be humbly questioned in order to gain reassurance that his repentance is sincere. The brethren must be careful to prove themselves as wise as serpents but as gentle as doves. In cases where the entire assembly is involved in the proceedings, any brethren who have factual knowledge which is plainly adverse to the restoration of the offender should bring that forth in a seasonable and proper manner.

The church and its officers are exercising proper caution when they question applicants for membership before admitting them. In like manner, they are within proper bounds to judiciously and graciously question a disciplined member before full restoration. This would be the case under any of the modes of discipline. However, when the case involves a private offence being dealt with privately, the offended person should be much less rigorous in demanding the marks of true repentance. Let his views of the other's words be generous and untainted by harshness of any kind. Love 'beareth all things, believeth all things, hopeth all things, endureth all things' [1 *Cor* 13:7]. Where discipline is undertaken in love, restoration will follow in like manner.

Conclusion

The history of God's people from Old Testament times up to the present day is one large collection of illustrations of the fact that the pathway to blessing is along the road of biblical truth. Certainly every faithful Christian desires God's glory, the prosperity of his church, and the welfare of every individual in that church. The Bible recognizes this threefold concern and biblical church discipline guards all three. So let us be taught of God and be leaders in the necessary reform of his church by being ready to govern and act according to his precepts and not our own fancy.

Appendix

What Our Protestant Forefathers Taught
Concerning Church Discipline

It would be easy to quote at length from some of the best Protestant pastors and theologians to show that they too believed substantially what has been presented in this booklet. However, it is of even greater value for us to consider what has been written on this subject in the leading Protestant creeds; for these creeds represent the mature insights of large groups of churches which on various occasions have called the best of their leaders together in order to state in writing exactly what they believed. Thus these creeds provide us with exact information concerning the way in which the mainstream of Protestantism has interpreted Scripture. If we ignore such testimony, it is to our own peril. The following documents do not exhaust the material, but are especially clear on the subject:

The Heidelberg Catechism was introduced into the churches and schools of Heidelberg, Germany in 1563. It has remained to this day a widely-used tool of instruction in Reformed Churches. In it we find the following:

'*Question 83*. What are the keys of the kingdom of heaven? [Matt 16:19].

Answer. The preaching of the holy gospel, and Christian discipline, or excommunication out of the Christian church; by these two, the kingdom of heaven is opened to believers, and shut against unbelievers.[*John* 21:23; *Matt* 18:15-18].

'*Question 84*. How is the kingdom of heaven opened and shut by the preaching of the holy gospel?

Answer. Thus: when, according to the command of Christ, it is declared and publicly testified to all and every believer, that whenever they receive the promise of the gospel by a true faith, all their sins are readily forgiven them of God, for the sake of Christ's merits; and on the contrary, when it is declared and testified to all unbelievers, and such as do not sincerely repent, that they stand exposed to the wrath of God, and eternal condemnation, so long as they are unconverted: according to which testimony of the gospel, God will judge them, both in this and the life to come. [*Matt* 28:19; *John* 3:18-36; *Mark* 16:15, 16; 2 *Thess* 1:7-9; *John* 20:21-23; *Matt* 16:19; *Rom* 2:2-17].

'*Question 85*. How is the kingdom of heaven shut and opened by Christian discipline?

Answer. Thus: when, according to the command of Christ, those who, under the name of Christians, maintain doctrines or practices inconsistent therewith, and will not, after having been brotherly admonished, renounce their errors and wicked course of life, are complained of to the church, or to those who are thereunto appointed by the church; and if they despise their admonition, are, by them, forbidden the use of the sacraments; whereby they are excluded from the Christian church, and by God Himself from the kingdom of Christ; and when they promise and show real amendment, are again received as members of Christ and His church. [*Matt* 18:15; 1 *Cor* 5:12; *Matt* 18:15-

18; *Rom* 12:7–10; 1 *Cor* 12:28; 1 *Tim* 5:17; 2 *Thess* 3:14; *Matt* 18:17; 1 *Cor* 5:3–5; 2 *Cor* 2:6–11; *Luke* 15:18]'.

One of the truly great Protestant creeds is *The Westminster Confession of Faith* completed in 1646. It is sometimes called the mother of all subsequent Reformed Confessions. Chapter XXX is entitled 'Of Church Censures' and reads as follows:

'I. The Lord Jesus, as King and Head of His church, hath therein appointed a government, in the hand of church officers, distinct from the civil magistrate.

'II. To these officers the keys of the kingdom of heaven are committed; by virtue whereof, they have power, respectively, to retain, and remit sins; to shut that kingdom against the impenitent, both by the Word, and censures; and to open it unto penitent sinners, by the ministry of the Gospel; and by absolution from censures, as occasion shall require.

'III. Church censures are necessary, for the reclaiming and gaining of offending brethren, for deterring of others from the like offences, for purging out of that leaven which might infect the whole lump, for vindicating the honour of Christ, and the holy profession of the gospel, and for preventing the wrath of God, which might justly fall upon the Church, if they should suffer His covenant, and the seals thereof, to be profaned by notorious and obstinate offenders.

'IV. For the better attaining of these ends, the officers of the church are to proceed by admonition, suspension from the sacrament of the Lord's Supper for a season; and by excommunication from the church, according to the nature of the crime, and demerit of the person.'

While the predominantly Presbyterian Westminster Assembly was meeting in England, the Congregationalists of New England were experiencing the need for a confession of faith of their own. So the leading Congretationalists met in Synod at Cambridge, Massachusetts, from 1646 to 1648. Desiring to demonstrate their substantial doctrinal agreement with their brethren in England, they adopted the Westminster Confession; 'Excepting only some sections in the 25, 30 and 31st chapters of their confession, which concern points of controversy in church-discipline; touching which we refer ourselves to the draft of church-discipline in the ensuing treatise.' Then they proceeded to offer a much more detailed statement of church-discipline than had been previously offered in a creed. The following is Chapter XIV of *The Cambridge Platform*, which is entitled 'Of Excommunication and Other Censures':

'I The censures of the church, are appointed by Christ, for the preventing, removing, and healing of offences in the church: for the reclaiming and gaining of offending brethen: for the deterring others from the like offences; for purging out the leaven which may infect the whole lump: for vindicating the honour of Christ, and of his church, and the holy profession of the gospel: and for preventing the wrath of God, that may justly fall upon the church, if they should suffer his covenant. and the seals thereof, to be profaned by notorious and obstinate offenders. [I *Tim* 5:20; *Deut* 17:12, 13; *Jude* 23; *Deut* 13:11; I *Cor* 5: 6; *Rom* 2:24; *Rev* 2:14, 15, 16, 20.]

'2 If an offence be private (one brother offending another) the offender is to go, and acknowledge his repentance for it unto his offended brother, who is then to forgive him, but if the offender neglect or refuse to do it, the brother offended is to go, and convince and admonish him of it, between themselves privately: if thereupon the offender be brought to repent of his offence, the admonisher hath won his brother, but if the offender hear not his brother, the brother offended is to take with him one or two more, that in the mouth of two or three witnesses, every word may be established (whether the word of admonition, if the offender receive it, or the word of complaint, if he refuse it): for if he refuse it, the offended brother is by the mouth of the elders to tell the church, and if he hear the church, and declare the same by penitent confession, he is recovered and gained; and if the church discern him to be willing to hear, yet not fully convinced of his offence, as in case of heresy; they are to dispense to him a public admonition; which declaring the offender to lie under the public offence of the church, doth thereby withhold or suspend him from the holy fellowship of the Lord's Supper, till his offence be removed by penitent confession. If he still continue obstinate, they are to cast him out by excommunication. [*Matt* 5:23, 24; *Luke* 17:3, 4; *Matt* 18:15–17; *Tit* 3:10]

'3 But if the offence be more public at first, and of a more heinous and criminal nature, to wit, such as are condemned by the light of nature; then the church without such gradual proceeding, is to cast out the offender from their holy communion, for the further mortifying of his sin and the healing of his soul, in the day of the Lord Jesus. [1 *Cor* 5:4, 5, 7].

'4 In dealing with an offender, great care is to be taken, that we be neither overstrict or rigorous, nor too indulgent or remiss; our proceeding herein ought to be with a spirit of meekness, considering ourselves, lest we also be tempted; and that the best of us have need of much forgiveness from the Lord. Yet the winning and healing of the offender's soul, being the end of these endeavours, we must not daub with untempered mortar, nor heal the wounds of our brethren slightly. On some have compassion, others save with fear. [*Gal* 6:1; *Matt* 18:34, 35; 6:14, 15; *Ezek* 13:10; *Jer* 6:14].

'5 While the offender remains excommunicate, the church is to refrain from all member-like communion with him in spiritual things, and also from all familiar communion with him in civil things, farther than the necessity of natural, or domestical, or civil relations do require: and are therefore to forbear to eat and drink with him, that he may be ashamed. [*Matt* 18:17; 1 *Cor* 5:11; 2 *Thess* 3:6, 14.]

'6 Excommunication being a spiritual punishment, it doth not prejudice the excommunicate in, nor deprive him of his civil rights, and therefore toucheth not princes, or other magistrates, in point of their civil dignity or authority. And, the excommunicate being but as a publican and a heathen, heathens being lawfully permitted to come to hear the Word in church assemblies, we acknowledge therefore the like liberty of hearing the Word, may be permitted to persons excommunicate that is permitted unto heathen. And because we are not without hope of his recovery, we are not to account him as an enemy but to admonish him as a brother. [1 Cor 14:24, 25; 2 Thess 3:14, 15.]

'7 If the Lord sanctify the censure to the offender, so as by the grace of Christ he doth testify his repentance, with humble confession of his sin, and judging of himself, giving glory unto God; the church is then to forgive him, and to comfort him, and to restore him to the wonted brotherly communion, which formerly he enjoyed with them. [2 Cor 2:7, 8.]

'8 The suffering of profane or scandalous livers to continue in fellowship, and partake in the sacraments, is doubtless a great sin in those that have power in their hands to redress it; and do it not. Nevertheless, inasmuch as Christ and his apostles in their times, and the prophets and other godly in theirs, did lawfully partake of the Lord's commanded ordinances in the Jewish church, and neither taught nor practised separation from the same, though unworthy ones were permitted therein; and inasmuch as the faithful in the church of Corinth, wherein were many unworthy persons, and practices, are never commanded to absent themselves from the sacraments, because of the same: therefore the godly in like cases, are not presently to separate. [Rev 2:14, 15, 20; Matt 23:3; Acts 3:1.]

'9 As separation from such a church wherein profane and scandalous livers are tolerated, is not presently necessary: so for the members thereof, otherwise worthy, hereupon to abstain from communicating with such a church, in the participation of the sacraments, is lawful. For as it were unreasonable, that a godly man should neglect duty, and punish himself in not coming for his portion in the blessing of the seals, as he ought, because others are suffered to come, that ought not, especially considering that himself doth neither consent to their sin, nor to their approaching to the ordinance in their sin, nor to the neglect of others who should put them away, and do not: but on the contrary doth heartily mourn for these things, modestly and seasonably stir up others to do their duty. If the church cannot be reformed, they may use their liberty, as is specified. But this all the godly are bound unto, even every one to do his endeavour, according to his power and place, that the unworthy may be duly proceeded against, by the church to whom this matter doth appertain. [2 *Chron* 30:18; *Gen* 18:25; *Ezek* 9:4; Chapter XIII, Section 4.]'

Some years later, the leading Congregationalists who had participated in the Westminster Assembly, along with some other notable Congregational leaders of England, met in a Synod to adopt a statement of faith. The result was *The Savoy Declaration of Faith and Order* which was simply *The Westminster Confession* with minor alterations, especially regarding church government. The following is their brief statement on church-discipline: (Last Chapter, Nos. 18 and 19).

'18 Whereas the Lord Jesus Christ hath appointed and instituted as a means of edification, that those who walk not according to the rules and laws appointed by him (in respect of faith and life, so that just offence doth arise to the church thereby) be censured in his name and authority. Every church hath power in itself to exercise and execute all those censures appointed by him in the way and order prescribed in the gospel.

'19 The censures so appointed by Christ, are admonition and excommunication. And whereas some offences are or may be known only to some, it is appointed by Christ, that those to whom they are so known, do first admonish the offender in private: in public offences where any sin, before all. And in the case of non-amendment upon private admonition, the offence being related to the church, and the offender not manifesting his repentance, he is to be duly admonished in the name of Christ by the whole church, by the ministry of the elders of the church; and if this censure prevail not for his repentance, then he is to be cast out by excommunication with the consent of the church.'

It should not be imagined that Protestants ever enjoyed the practice of censuring their church members, but nevertheless they have generally recognized it as a necessary function of the church. If any are still contentious against this biblical practice we can only say, as Moses did to Israel, 'Your murmurings are not against us, but against the Lord' [*Exodus* 16:8].

For Further Reading

Bannerman, James, *The Church of Christ,* Vol. 2, pp. 186–200. Reprinted Banner of Truth Trust, 1974.

Baxter, Richard, *The Reformed Pastor,* pp. 104–111, 163–171. Reprinted Banner of Truth Trust, 1974.

Calvin, John, *Institutes of the Christian Religion,* Book IV, Chapter XII, Section 1–13.

Edwards, Jonathan, 'The Nature and End of Excommunication,' *Works,* Vol. II, pp. 118–121. Reprinted Banner of Truth Trust, 1974.

Mack, Wayne, *The Biblical Concept of Church Discipline,* Cherry Hill, New Jersey: Mack Publishing Company, 1974.

Owen, John, *Of Excommunication, Works,* Vol. XVI, pp. 151–183. Reprinted Banner of Truth Trust, 1968.

PRINTED AND BOUND IN ENGLAND BY
HAZELL WATSON AND VINEY LTD, AYLESBURY, BUCKS